Denis Laming

Denis Laming
Invisible Tensions

Edited by
Maurizio Vitta

l'ARCAEDIZIONI

Photographic Credits

Luc Boegly
Michel Denancé
Alain Gouillardon
Denis Laming
Bernard Regent
Sylva Villerot
Marc Vimenet

Editorial Director USA
Pierantonio Giacoppo

Chief Editor of Collection
Maurizio Vitta

Publishing Coordinator
Franca Rottola

Graphic Design
Stefano Tosi

Translation and Editing
Martin J. Anderson

Colour-separation
Chromia, Meda

Printing
Poligrafiche Bolis, Bergamo

First published October 1999

ISBN 88-7838-054-7

Contents

Introduction

by Maurizio Vitta

As we well know, modern-day architecture gave up the idea of representing its own contents some time ago, preferring instead to just represent itself. Self-reference is now the norm: after first feeding on ideology and then history, architecture has ended up mirroring itself and nothing else.

The historians of the future will have to analyse the real nature of this "self-reflection". On a superficial level it seems to be full of negative connotations - buildings are reduced to mere images, physical embodiments of the architect's "artistry", with architecture guilty of lapsing into a form of stage design or, worse still, narcissism. But this is not the only way of looking at things: a lot of modern buildings have managed to re-knit the urban fabric surrounding them, creating a new kind of awareness projecting them onto a common plane of aesthetic values and social expectations. There is nothing fundamentally wrong with this general analysis, although it lacks the kind of penetrating critical insight that would cast some real light on the actual forces in play in contemporary architectural design. Commentary never rises up to the level of criticism, while criticism itself is largely ignored by history.

Nevertheless, as the cultural adventure of the XXth century draws to a close, criticism must provide the starting point not just for writing history, but for laying the foundations for future developments. In this respect Denis Laming's work is a privileged testing ground, containing all the necessary ingredients for defining the conceptual structure of XXth century architecture and, *in nuce*, providing the means of envisaging the potential scenarios of the next few decades.

A disturbingly original event stands out in Laming's work: the construction of Futuroscope Park in Poitiers. Original because it grounds an experience that projects well beyond its own boundaries; disturbing because it is all condensed in one single point. The premises underpinning Futuroscope Park already embraced the guiding principles of contemporary architecture: the concept of "image" epitomised by the very nature of an exhibition-education "park"; a sense of projection into the future designed around the twentieth-century notion of progress as a deliberate "breaking" with the past; a feeling for the "virtual" nature of reality, blocked on the threshold separating the concreteness of things from their transparent electronic embodiment.

Futuroscope Park works around the idea of reducing architecture - its premises, spaces, structures, and furbishing - to the status of a mere "icon". The client made his intentions quite clear in this respect. Considering the Park was only supposed to provide "images" of things, its functional layout had to be turned into an "image" itself, or rather the "image of an image". Architecture needed to embody a concept rather than a function. In other words, it had to regain hold of its old ideological groundings but without ideology itself, which was now replaced by faith in progress through the possibilities opened up by technology.

In this respect Laming was working in the mainstream of late twentieth-century Western architecture. The replacing of ideological pretensions with technological optimism marked the twilight of utopia and the dawning of a new virtual age that merely copies reality without contrasting it; and it is architecture that must transform this into a perceptual (the "icon") and spatio-temporal (functional structures) experience. Laming was also asked to bring out the way in which this might be effected by injecting his park with an implicit sense of spectacle.

The key to Laming's success is the way he has carefully avoided the trap of simply translating a concept into an image. Rather then merely creating spectacular architecture he has actually set architecture on the stage, making it a paradigm of cultural change. He took the idea of the future in the making as the absolute limit of the historical scenario we have already left behind, but whose fiery breadth can still be felt on our necks. He has marked this limit through an eruption of forms that seems to be teetering on the brink of the future and all the exciting prospects it has to offer. But at the same time he has also been careful not to go any further and cross the threshold beyond which architectural measure and control are forced to dissolve into the misty realms of vaticination, where art alone is free to follow its own whims.

What Laming has managed to do is to design aesthetically daring architectural structures that are firmly grounded in our culture.

We cannot help noting how the dazzling brilliance of the intriguing figures of the Futuroscope buildings is geared to simple geometric figures - either flat like a circle, square and triangle, or as solid as a sphere, cylinder and prism. These traditional solid forms somehow recreate the basic forms of nature, such as crystals, or emulate the undulations and vibrant reflections of the water in which they are reflected here and there. Euclidean geometry and natura naturans reign supreme in buildings designed to be "icons" of a technological future. But all this is carefully calculated: it links up with the intrinsic qualities of architecture, its role in determining how we physically and symbolically experience space, and its sense of history as movement and, at the same time, permanence.

Having effected this structural minimisation of architecture, Laming then proves that it is not up to the new tasks at hand. The idea that "simple forms" guarantee the creation of beautiful constructions is fading away along with the twentieth century, as science shows even more clearly than architecture. Fractal mathematics and chaos theory have already shown how beauty in nature derives from a combination of order and disorder. This is why Benoît Mandelbrot considered simple forms to be "inhuman" and compared the Seagram Building to Beaux-Arts architecture which rejects unity of scale as its compositional structure quite literally expands out before our very eyes. These concepts can only be grounded in architecture once they have been stripped of all decoration and projected into the focal point of design. The model to be emulated is not XIXth century eclecticism but rather XVIIth century Baroque with its deep and elegant sense of sudden contrast, unexpected oxymorons, and metaphors that open up the mind to new visions. There is actually a structural sense of disorder in

Baroque architecture as it tends towards even greater order, grounding its logical forms in complexity, a multiplicity of different perspectives, *trompe-l'oeils*, and transient-illusory spaces.

These cultural connotations emerge in various different ways at Futuroscope depending on the function and nature of the buildings. Viewing his architectural work in its entirety, its true force only really emerges where it seems most vulnerable, or in other words in its spectacularity and scenographic power. Sheer architectural "staging" creates the kind of effects that Baroque culture gave to art: that so-called "*meraviglia*", not just the kind of astonishment we experience when we see something new which soon becomes quite familiar, but the sense of bewilderment evoked when discovering that reality can only be as it appears and realising that knowledge of this fact will change us forever. This is not just a simple idea of "the world as a spectacle", an illusory panopticon of vane shadows projected on a screen. It is really the typically Baroque idea of "the whole world being a stage" on which certainty and illusion co-exist in a permanent state of conflict whose outcome remains a mystery. In some way this is the same idea as Oklahoma Theater in Franz Kafka's *America*, where everyone is encouraged to try their hand at acting: "If you want to be an artist, join our company! Our theater can find employment for everyone, a place for everyone". But crossing that threshold does not necessarily mean moving out of the real world into the theatre. The opposite might happen, since this is "the biggest theatre in the world" and all those who have seen it "say that there are almost no limits to it".

The spectacularity underpinning how Futuroscope works also underlies its architecture that treats this sense of spectacle more as a conceptual notion than a design strategy. The idea of basing the architectural forms on simple geometric figures is not so much designed to strike the imagination as to use the imagination as a logical guideline or heuristic device. The disorder is carefully constructed; if anything, it is the order it creates that is really surprising.

This is even more true in the case of a complex that takes science projected towards the future as its focal point. The revolutionary, enlightened architecture of Ledoux and Boullée is sometimes mentioned in relation to Futuroscope Park, and rightly so: but only in connection with the stylistic side of the project. Laming was not trying to either express a vision of some new society or a powerful yearning to leave a trace on history. Newton's cenotaph celebrated the triumph of organised thought; Chaux's ideal city transformed that symbol into a social model. Modern science shows no sign of this confidence, which has in fact now been delegated to technology with the same kind of nonchalance that a nobleman gives away an old suit to his servant as a present. If anything we can sense how a tormented old system can see the chance of fresh knowledge in its own collapse. This is how Tommaso Campanella built his own Sun City as a revolutionary utopia in which science really had the task of bitterly criticising the old order rather than celebrating the new order that was taking its place. Laming's Futuroscope Park expresses the sheer energy of scientific thought capable of controlling matter, as well as the uncertainty as to how it is to handle this control. These faceted architectural structures, that cannot be taken in at a glance, embrace both the possibilities and uncertainties that the future inevitably holds, and, in any case, are open

to whatever course mankind chooses to take.

The standard of the rest of Denis Laming's work proves that these are the real contents of his architecture. The design philosophy of Futuroscope Park in Poitiers is further embodied in other similar works, such as the Imax 3D Theater in Denver, the Boeing Imax 3D Theater in Seattle or Shanghai Scienceland. This underlying philosophy is, however, much more contained, carefully managing to keep image implicit and architectural content explicit. Elsewhere, as in the Catholic University in La Roche-sur-Yon, the Omnivest Business Park in Denver or Omnivest International Headquarters, again in Denver, architecture gains the upper hand. In other words it becomes an "image" of itself, without ever losing sight of the fact that its success lies in a delicate balance between artistry and reason.

This clearly emerges from Laming's latest design for a European Ecumenical Center for the Study of Religious Images in Poitiers. Architecture turns into image ready to be converted into pure symbolic space: the building is actually structured around the idea of transcendence so that its structures and spaces project an immanent sense of tension. More than anywhere else this Center transmits a sense of those "invisible tensions" on which Laming has grounded his basic approach to design.

Laming tells us that "the architect must have a spectral view of things". In other words he must reduce reality to appearance and grasp the truth that he can glimpse behind it. It is worth remembering that modern art drew its innovative force from this desire to go beyond perception. Rimbaud described the poet as a "voyant"; Cézanne saw "the dark side of things" and for Kandinsky the artist "sees and indicates". A vision of the invisible was a real imperative for a form of

art that yearned to say what cannot be said and express the ineffable.

Architecture cannot take this same path, but it can let the same tension flow through its structures. This tension will have to work inside its cavities, in the gaps between its materials, in those dark areas where space fades into nothing. It will have to focus on the contrast between the whole and its parts, between the structure closed within itself and the fragmentation that breaks this unity, resolving these antinomies through conflict rather than reconciliation. This re-evokes the old conflict between form and function, but it also brings out with great force the contrast between image and form, concept and image, and design as graphic "representation" against concept as phenomenological "representation". Unlike art, it brings a total experience into play in which these contrasts are simultaneously imposed, and to do this it has to focus on changes in its hierarchical orders to express its own internal dynamics.

In this Derridian perspective, which is quite indifferent to the enticements of architectural "deconstructivism", Denis Laming has found his own important yet eccentric place. Although his most recent batch of works is still closely linked to the underlying premises that motivated Futuroscope Park, they are much more richly nourished. The differences - marking a gradual evolution - predominantly involve the icons of architecture. The building at Roche-sur-Yon features a segmentation of structures in an alternating combination of linearity and undulation, continuity and rupture; at Shanghai, the structures flatten out and turn transparent, abandoning the opacity of matter so that we can gaze through it; the geometrical forms of the Seattle project are clear-cut and rhythmically patterned out in a continuous perspective that is only interrupted by the solid mass of the sphere wedged inside; the Imax 3D Theater in Denver is a synthetic rendering of the Poitiers design, while the Omnivest Headquarters rejects Euclidean geometry to venture into fractals.

Order and disorder interact on almost conflicting terms: each architectural feature is like a sort of micro-system, but the overall structure breaks down logical relations to reproject them on different, distant levels. Even the relations between vertical and horizontal planes begin to waver uneasily. The constructions appear to be rooted to the ground, since the architecture actually seems to be styled around the idea of flattening them to the ground. But, at the same time, they thrust upwards as if to break free from their own weightiness. We are suddenly confronted with another opposition, symbolised by the binary combination of ground/air and its conceptual counterpart of transcendence/immanence, that takes us to the very limits of dialectical design.

These tensions, which are not actually embodied in architectural "image" but can be sensed through other means than visual perception, are really incursions into a dimension of time that is neither the present nor the future. It is as if they were searching for a "temporal dimension" which architecture (and works of art in general) can only create by enveloping itself in everyday reality and by running the risk of confronting a notion of time that belongs not to history but to the very experience of life (Husserl's notion of *Erlebnis*, if you like). The concept of the future, which Denis Laming also focus on, is not confined to envisaging (and hence willing) what will necessarily emerge from a set of premises based on the present (as in the case of Futurist ideology). It is much closer to Bergson's idea of "duration", which is at once memory, vital force and intuition, and so not a "measurable" form of time or, as Bergson himself would say, "spatialised" time.

Of course this kind of reading applies to most of contemporary architecture. But Laming's works openly invoke it by calling directly into question the problem of "icons" and hence the relation between "architectural" image and "representation". Whereas the Futuroscope project solved the problem in favour of the former (since the project brief posed it in functional terms), subsequent works mainly focused on the latter, injecting a larger dose of semantic force to compensate for the reduction in visual impact. In any case the whole issue is now a sort of conceptual leit-motif on which Laming will certainly be able to ground his forthcoming works.

But this does not mean that the problem has been dealt with. Denis Laming's work draws attention to the issues raised by a certain ideological void in architectural practice. Ideology certainly was not the answer - it never has been - but it did at least point out the need for architectural design to be more closely knit into society and culture as a whole. Ideology did not need to be kept to at all costs: even opposition, transgression, and just flatly saying "no" had their own particular sense, direction, and prospects. In the wake of socio-cultural planning, architecture - like all art in general - found itself at grips with pure "images" lacking in "representation" and was therefore forced to come to terms with itself alone. This is not such a bad thing: there is no reason why this should not provide a solution to what is now a rather tricky problem. If this happens to be the case, then everyone must play their part.

Architects like Denis Laming will be left the job of rising just far enough above their own designs to catch a glimpse of even wider horizons. It is not just architecture that is being shaken by "invisible tensions", we can all eel them: what we really need are "images" capable of "representing them" properly.

Works

Futuroscope Park

Poitiers, France

Futuroscope Park, built between 1984 and 1996, is designed for a specific purpose: to provide a setting for the future and cast some light on times to come so that we can scrutinise its forms, structures, lifestyles, and possible or theoretically feasible activities in what might be described as "our descendants' present". The idea of an observatory had to be gauged to that of a stage. This kind of setting does not reject analysis, it takes it to its logical extreme, so that it takes on the force of a pure image.

Stretching over a surface area of 170 hectares in the heart of a cereal/corn-growing region in the Department of Vienne, Futuroscope Park was commissioned with great insistence by the regional authorities. The competition organised in 1984 was won by Denis Laming's design, which was judged to have interpreted the spirit of the project better than all the rest.

Laming set about disorienting visitors, who were immediately faced with a kind of reality given concrete form by architecture on a visionary scale. The "non-contemporary" design of this architectural scene had to physically embody this gap in time so that the future could be contemplated in an "image" capable of conveying a quivering threshold between the present and future. Working on a clever interplay of simple geometric forms - solids and structures of a distinctly

Euclidean nature - Laming has injected architectural space with the same bewildering sense of distance in time that the teaching and exhibition facilities inside the various buildings transmit on a daily basis.

The Futuroscope Pavilion, after which the entire Park was then named, has been described as a "window on the future". Its architecture plays entirely on simple geometric forms - the sphere and prism - as if to emphasise how Euclidean geometry can get its own back on the fancy techniques used to express its construction/functional features. The rituals of science and new technology are celebrated inside.

The three-dimensional nature of naturalistic philosophy suddenly gives way to the overwhelming stylistic complexity of the Kinemax that breaks down the feeling of security associated with earthly spatial relations and develops into structures that seem to re-echo the most startling ideas dreamed up by H.P. Lovecraft, but which actually convert the mathematical discoveries of our day into architectural forms. On the other hand, the spatial ambiguity of the Omnimax tends to test out classical geometry by projecting simple figures like the cube and sphere into a state of imbalance.

Whereas the Tapis Magique (Magic Carpet) is just a structural form in space, more sculptural than architectural, the Imax® 3D draws more heavily on modern

architectural idiom, emphasising its inherent sense of progress to create a construction that projects into the future and, at the same time, epitomises the state of contemporary design. Elsewhere, such as in the Institute of Perspective, we are faced with the architectural camouflaging of the latest scientific technology, while the National Center for Distance Teaching uses architectural symbolism to create a form of triangular incision that breaks up a regular rectangular design and calls to mind the incision Epharistos cut in Zeus's head from which Athens, the goddess of knowledge, was spawned. The lenticular layout of Lentille, a building providing accommodation for 132 students, is designed to reflect Western culture's obsession with light.

The TGV station provides an ideal conclusion to the overall architectural complex by the way it intrinsically represents speed - a modern myth that the XXth century exalts through space and which the future will probably commemorate in time.

Futuroscope Pavilion

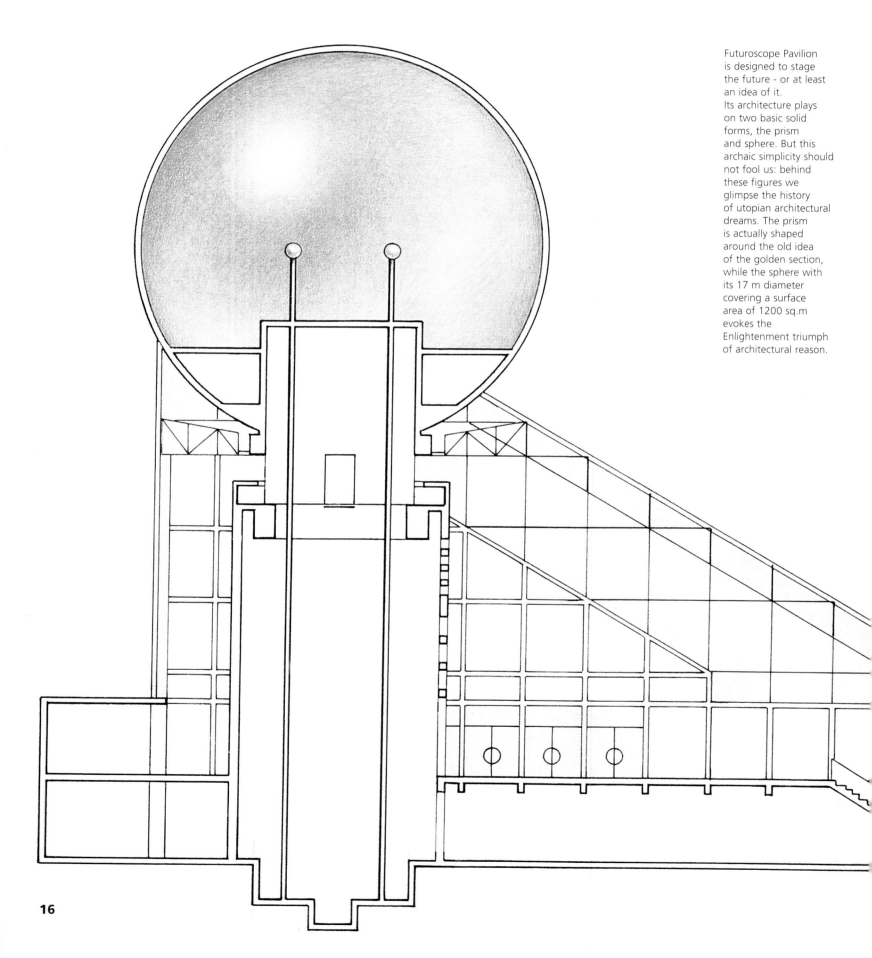

Futuroscope Pavilion is designed to stage the future - or at least an idea of it. Its architecture plays on two basic solid forms, the prism and sphere. But this archaic simplicity should not fool us: behind these figures we glimpse the history of utopian architectural dreams. The prism is actually shaped around the old idea of the golden section, while the sphere with its 17 m diameter covering a surface area of 1200 sq.m evokes the Enlightenment triumph of architectural reason.

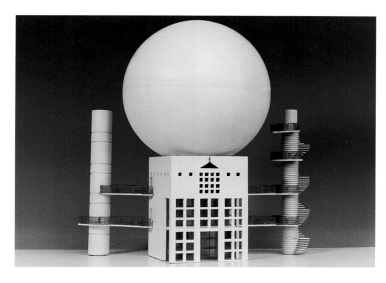

The entrance to Futuroscope Pavilion is underground to create greater dialectical interaction between the past and future, subtely expressed by Denis Laming's architecture. The structure of the building is an articulated system of cultural references, where the sun rises over a world in mutation.

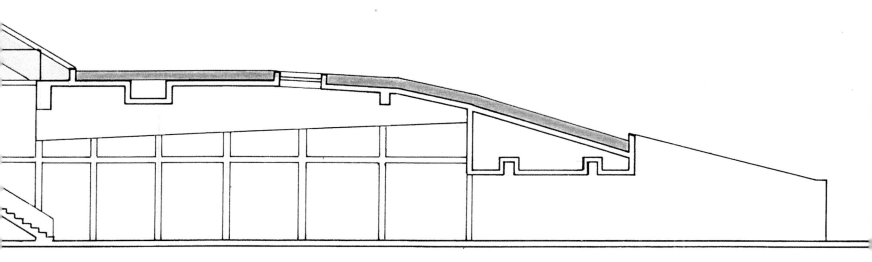

2

Kinemax

The profile of the Kinemax - hosting the first Imax theater in France - aims to represent the kind of "spin" and visual communication on which much of our culture is grounded. Its crystalline profile evokes the issue of complexity; but its transparency and the kaleidoscopic flow of its structures allude to the ambiguous nature of contemporary knowledge, hovering on the brink of reality and virtuality.

The building is formed by a granite base and a hexagonal mirrored superstructure. It houses an airtight waterproof enclosure. This dual system, implemented by Denis Laming in other theater designs, enhances a tremendous visual impact while keeping down construction and maintenance costs. So as not to shatter the dream of the end of the film, the screen rises and visitors are attracted by the immaterial vision of the lake.

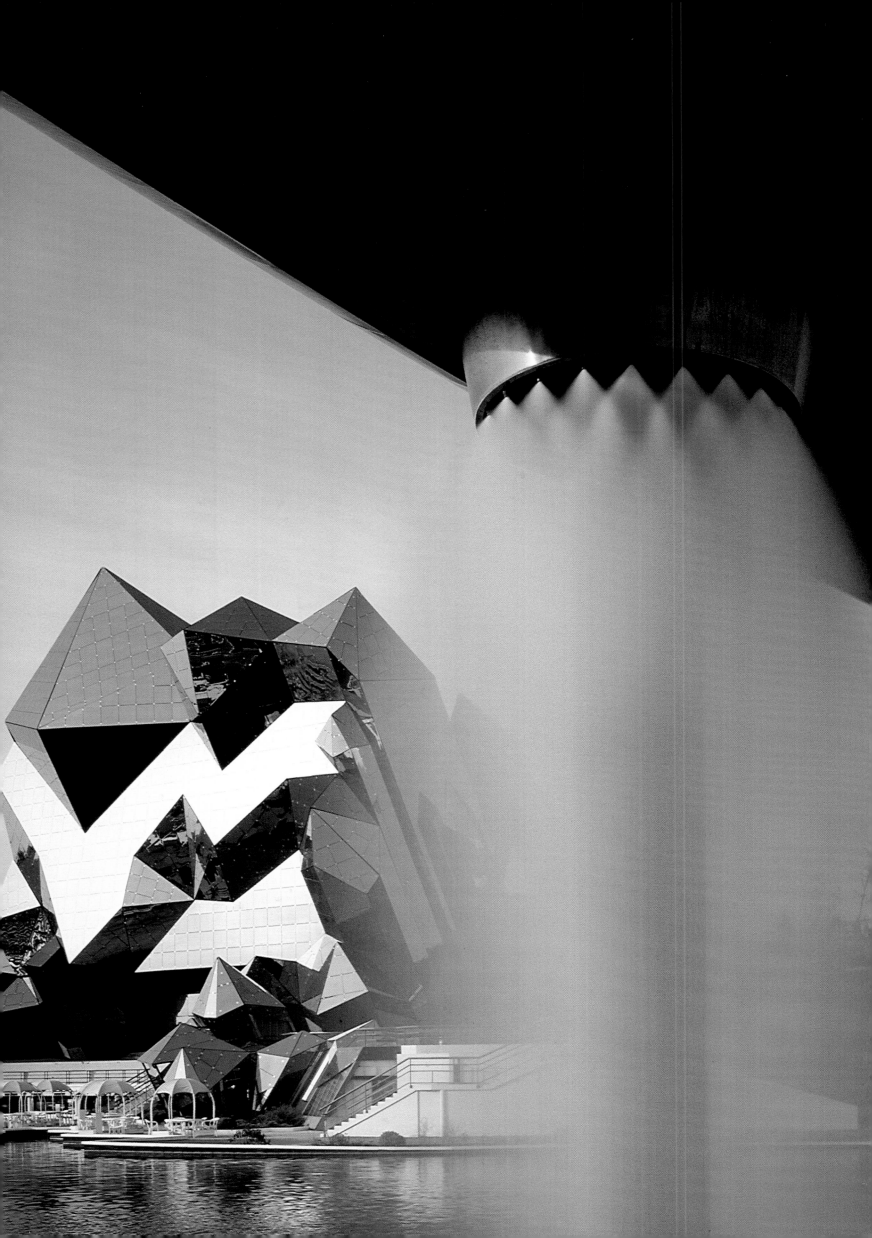

Omnimax

3

The Omnimax takes up the dialectical relations between a sphere and prismatic solids - in this case a cube - relaunching the issue in the dramatic context of interaction with the ground. The two volumes are composed so that, depending on the lighting, one could be more present than the other. The intensity of the sun and the presence of clouds let each form appear on its own. Reflections of one play on the other thus permitting volumetric variations. In this way, the optimal visual effect is achieved while minimizing construction costs.

The sphere has a metallic aspect and the cube is made of semi-reflecting glass. The cube symbolizes rationality, the sphere irrationality or the spiritual. Joined together they evoke the imaginary which becomes reality.

4

Vienne Pavilion and Magic Carpet

Water is a vital element in the design of the whole of Futuroscope Park. The Vienne Pavilion and Magic Carpet underline its symbolic function. The building stands along the lake side as an immaterial cathedral, a fountain of petrified light reflecting in the lake. The facade, vertical tubes of varying height, evoke the fiber optics and cables which equip the park. The tubes shift from reflecting to translucent and then transparent in order to reinforce the fervour of the building. Its bevelled mirrors at the top are like eyes scanning the sky, peering into the future, and listening to the cosmos.

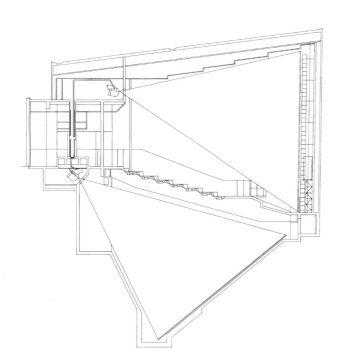

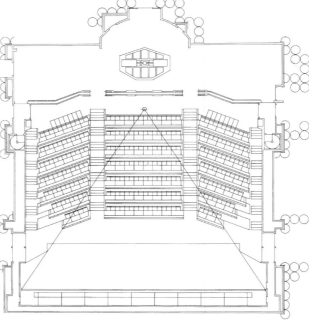

The "pipes" of the Magic Carpet contain a projection room designed to hold the Double Imax System. Water represents the fluidity and purity of information, whose simple exterior hides the complexity of the internal ties between the different elements which it composes.

5

Imax® 3D

The facade is constructed out of a glass wall in one single piece, 25 m tall and 35 m wide. A huge circular concave form deforms the facade's flat surface like a lens, designing an excavated relief in which the world is turned upside down. A semi-sphere clad with a smooth metal skin seems to be gravitating. The image evoked is that of a planet revolving around a star that holds it in its gravitational field. 3D films, which can only be viewed wearing goggles made of polarizing glass, are projected on a flat screen inside the hall.

6

International Prospective Institute

The central structure of the Prospective Institute draws on dome-shaped and panoptic forms, as well as the stylistic techniques at the very roots of modern architecture.

Here architecture openly avows its tangential relations with art and sculpture in particular, since it creates a sculpted "object" capable of holding a series of spaces designed for science and research purposes. Petals "protect" researchers, from exposure to daily constraints.

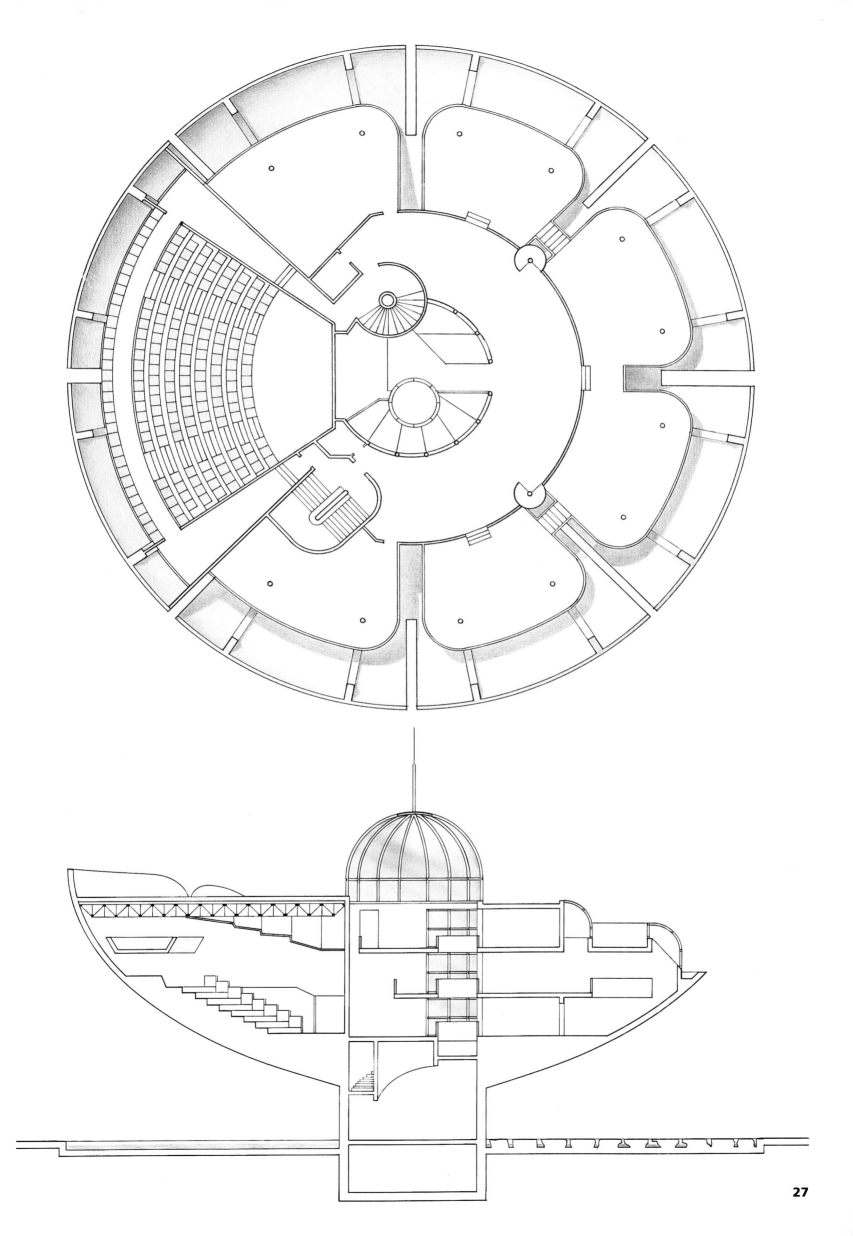

The Institute of Prospective's architecture plays on the idea of a parabola bursting out of a pool of water. This form multiplies its semantic energy through geometry until it reaches technology and then, eventually, an idea of nature expressed in the image of a lotus flower symbolising harmony and creativity.

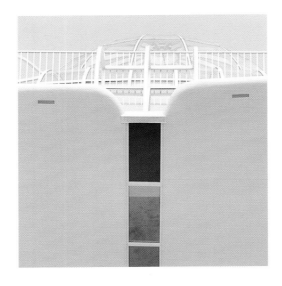

The "great theater of the world" is a Baroque concept that Futuroscope's architecture physically embodies as both image and functional space.

7

Multimedia Center

Multi-media technology - an idealised concept in contemporary culture - is given its most austere rendering here, as allusions to the history of XXth century architecture are converted into signs of a transformation based on a certain harsh, conflictual notion of continuity, but no permanent rupture with the past.

The basic simplicity
of the structures
betrays the complexity
of the architectural
design which, inside the
building, is transformed
into a carefully
designed environment.

8

Teleport

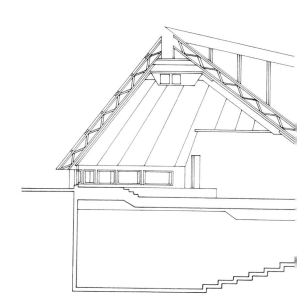

The Futuroscope Teleport is a keystone to the site and its future development. It was designed to act as a switchboard to the park, education and business sectors. It is a major site for receiving high definition television images (HDTV) notably the retransmission of Albertville Winter Olympics and the live showing of the Barcelona Summer Olympics. It is connected via optic fibers to the education and business districts and was the first place in France where two-way video transmissions are perceived.

The Telecommunications Center was built in 1989 around a hallowed core which symbolizes the fact that communications are invisible and only their impact can be perceived. Its 1,600 sq.m are comprised of several levels including a control studio, a screening room with seating for 180, conference and exhibition halls, videotransmission and videocom rooms, and a space where France Telecom showcases its products.

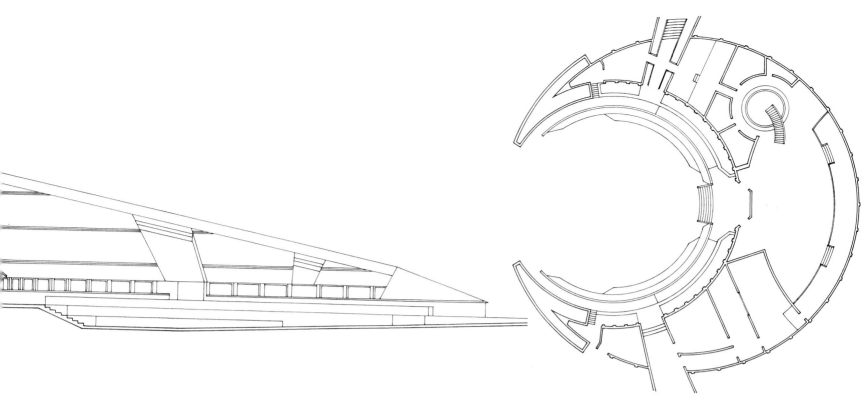

Once again the dialectical relations between interior and exterior, solids and voids, concept and matter, are physically embodied in a structure that takes on these meanings to convert them into function, service and message.

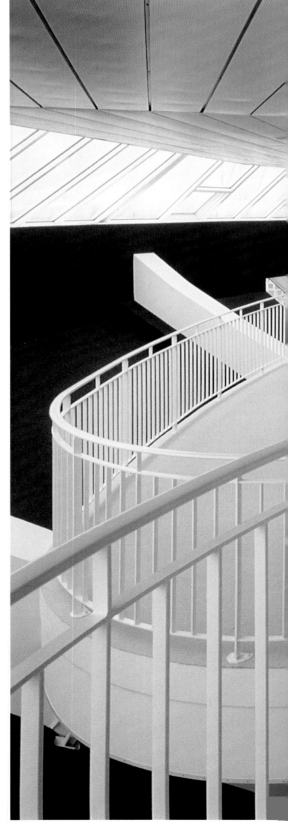

9

Physics Education and Research Center

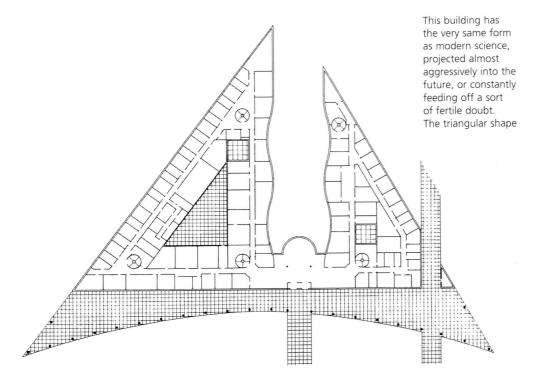

This building has the very same form as modern science, projected almost aggressively into the future, or constantly feeding off a sort of fertile doubt. The triangular shape of the building plan immediately alludes to the origins of geometry, but the horizontal openings of the facade, featuring an alternating combination of transparency and opacity, warn us against over-confiding in scientific optimism which needs to be confronted with a sort of complexity which is extremely hard to control.

The strictly technological nature of the structure turns the grounding architectural concept of a building designed to express how measure and imagination interrelate into an aesthetic experience.

10 Conference Center

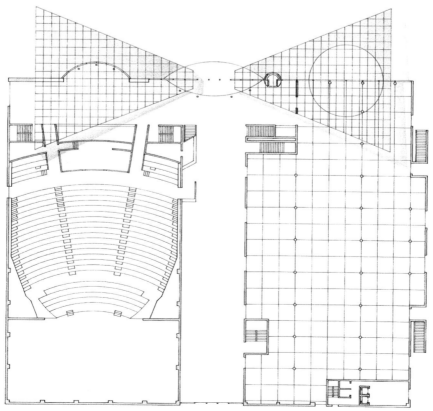

In a building designed to relate, exchange and interact, architectural signs abound, creating a clever semantic network mirroring the openings, communicative force and spirit of cooperation characterising modern culture. The sphere, which crops up again here as a conceptual component of the architecture, conveys the image of world in which peace has given way to direct confrontation between science and ethics.

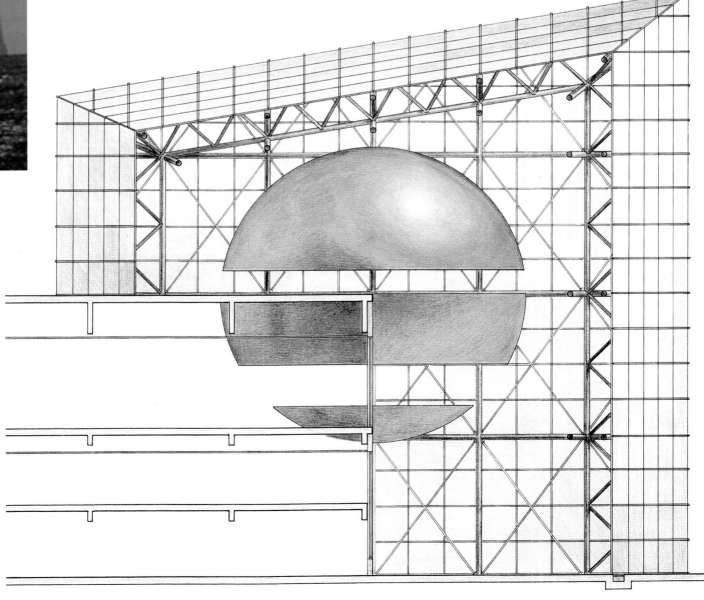

The incisive nature of technological image and its transparency emphasise the building's function which the interiors embody in a vision of the continuity of XXth and XXIst century architecture. Made of semi-reflective glass and therefore semi-transparent, it reveals part of the internal structure. The right-hand prism can be seen to hold a sphere enclosing the restaurant.

The butterfly-wing site plan is organised around a central road and large naturally-lit hall. The left wing contains a 1200-seat amphitheater. The right wing holds an exhibition hall and restaurant catering for over one thousand diners.

11

Lentille

Designed to host
accommodation,
the Lentille is an
urbanistic component
of Futuroscope Park:
it underlines a kind
of architectural quality
capable of modulating
its semantic energy
to the various functions
of the Park's intricate
layout.

In the Lentille project, there is a reversal in the relations between vertical image (the building's "presence" in the environment) and horizontal image (the plan with its functional layout of spaces) in the other buildings: the site plan is more streamlined and expressive compared to the stylistic balance of the facades.

The lines of force and the perimeter of the building are developed along the alignment of the buildings along the road and correspond to a very high-density urban layout.

The general form of the building is similar to a convex lens, in which the focal point is a void to leave room for an open terrace. The internal distribution, the partition walls and the infrastructures containing utilities are designed to be gradually altered. The main principle is that of two lodgings inscribing a common space. Thanks to an interplay of double partitions and openings a single apartment can be adapted into a double or triple one.

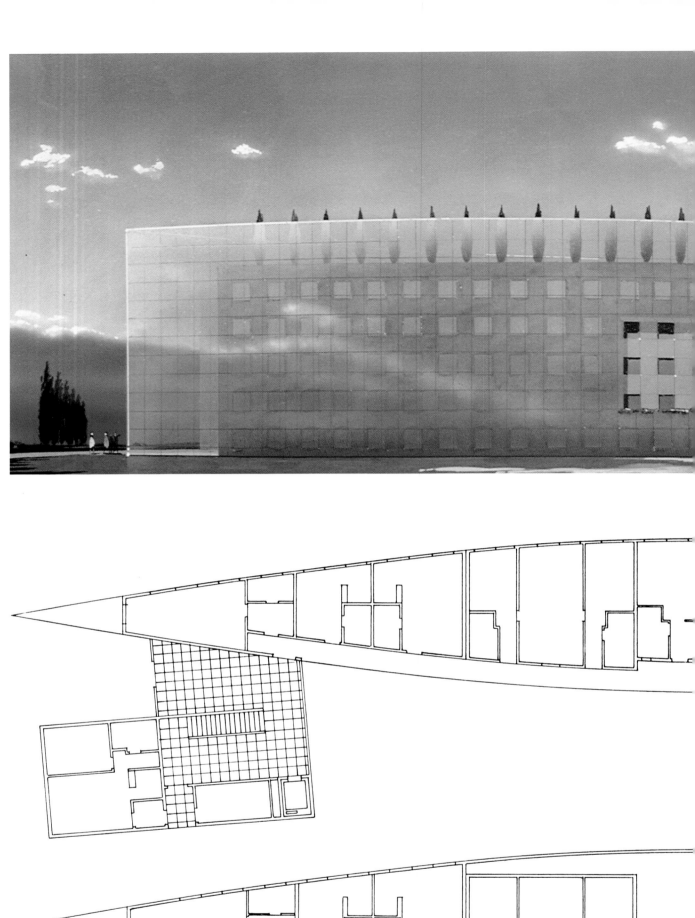

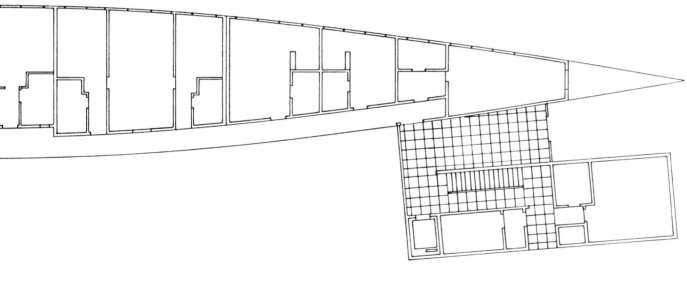

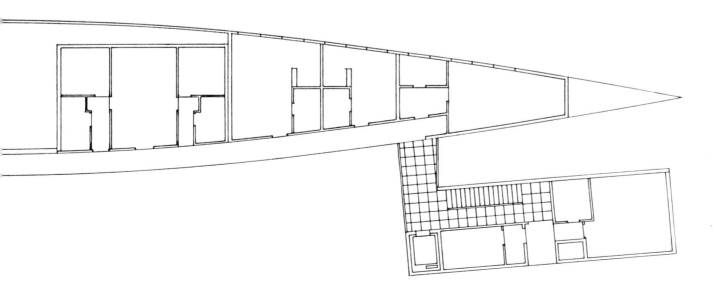

12

National Tele-learning Center

This office building houses the headquarters of the National Tele-learning Center Cegetel, TDR and Galleries Lafayette. Situated right at the entrance, the three office buildings are key architectural features of the entire Futuroscope area. Like the "Pylos" of Egyptian temples, they stand guard at "the city gates". This effect is brought out by their geometric forms and height.

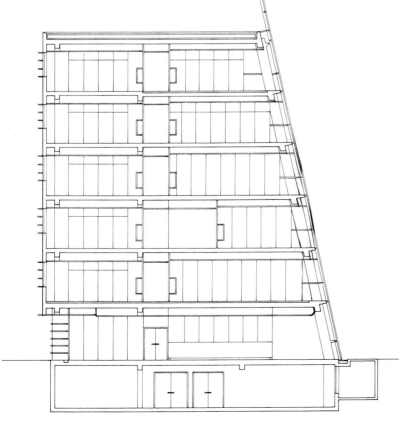

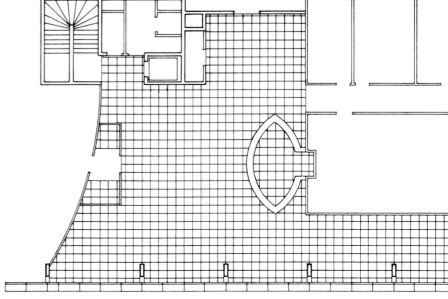

This building is, above all, a town-planning feature, given its position at the entrance to Futuroscope Park. The structure's high-tech image, underlined by the huge sloping facade, vigorously embodies the cultural nature of its destination, reinforced on the inside by cross-paths overlooking both sides and by flexible use of spaces.

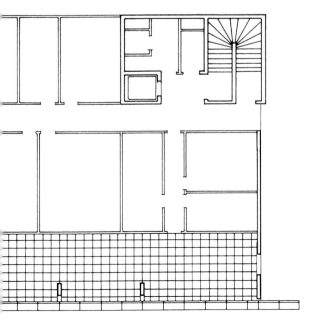

13 TGV Station

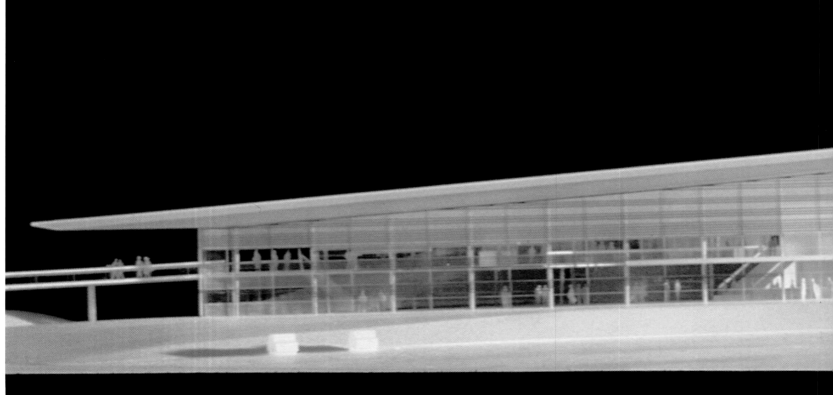

Futuroscope Park is connected to the SNCF, and the station marks the junction of two technological moments - image and communication - embodied in an architectural design playing heavily on an intricate interplay of triangles. The building's main functions are spread over two levels: services and a luggage deposit on the ground floor; facilities belonging to Futuroscope Park, SNCF waiting rooms, and a system of shops on the top floor.

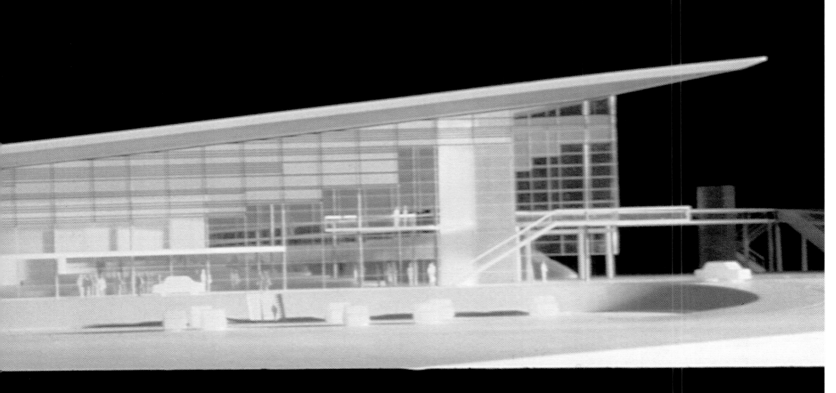

The station is designed to allow the eight-hundred visitors getting off the train to flow in and out of Futuroscope Park as easily as possible. This is made possible by a system of gently sloping ramps and by the stylistic lines of the architectural design.

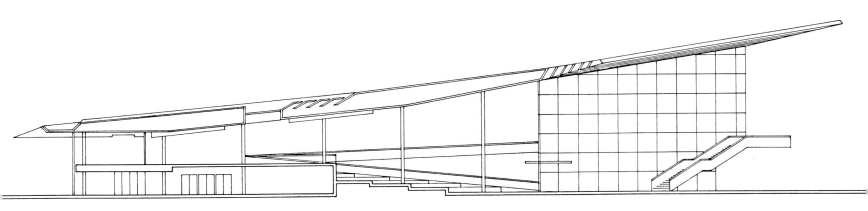

The building's triangular design allows one of the sides to be straight and parallel to the tracks, the other side to provide access to the pedestrian walkway, and the hypotenuse to ensure transition from one world to the other.

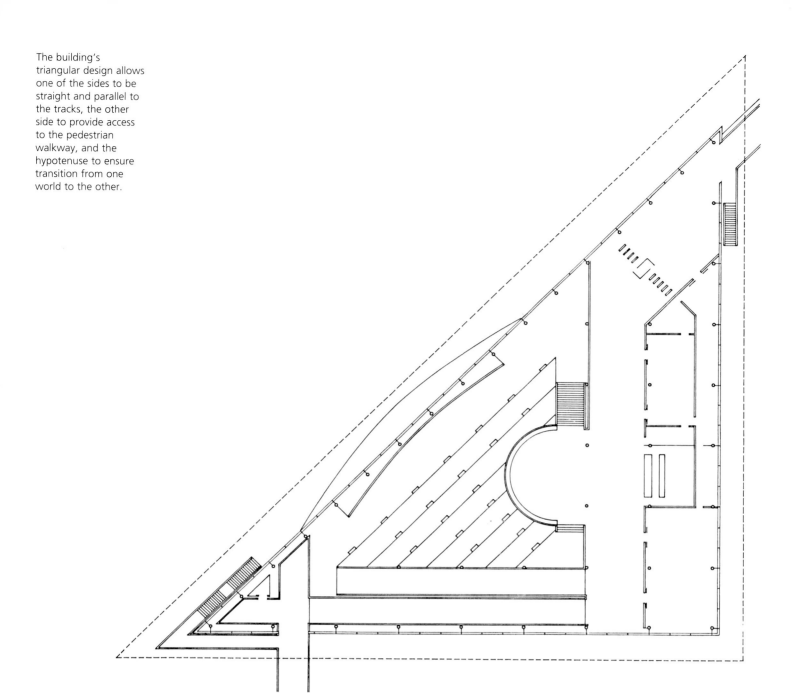

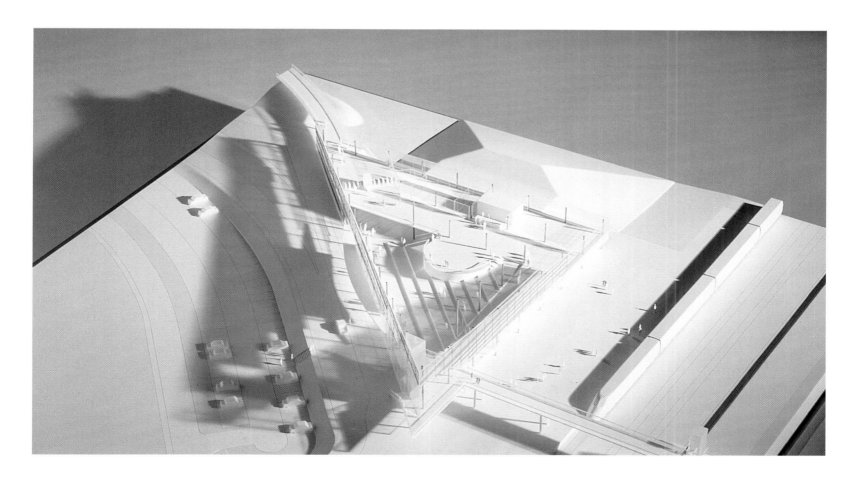

Catholic University and Library

La Roche-sur-Yon, France

Built along the Boulevard Circulaire, this new building belonging to the Catholic University helps structurally organise the city's urban development scheme, stitching into it nicely.

The main facade along the boulevard has an undulating design featuring two tympanums: one made of stone representing the rigour of a Cartesian world, and the other made of different types of glass symbolising the mystery and profundity of Faith. The suspended fixture whose light, undulating form slips in between these two architectural features evokes the passage of time.

Although it was actually constructed in three stages, the overall design has lost none of the rigour of the basic design.

The structure hinges around a central opening leading to the entrances and vertical circulation facilities, as well as guiding visitors through the building with the help of its luminous perspectives. The large well-lit lobby opens up on one side and the amphitheaters over on the other. There is a small circular amphitheater in the middle, where students can congregate and socialise.

The overall design communicates a sense of great tranquillity and is bound to create a place where young people can get together and interact in relaxing surroundings.

The library in the south part of the complex has a square building plan with a large arch in front of it that harks back to the tympanums on the facade. It also lets through just the right amount and quality of light, as the ICES's plastic architectural design actually seems to be winking at the outside world.

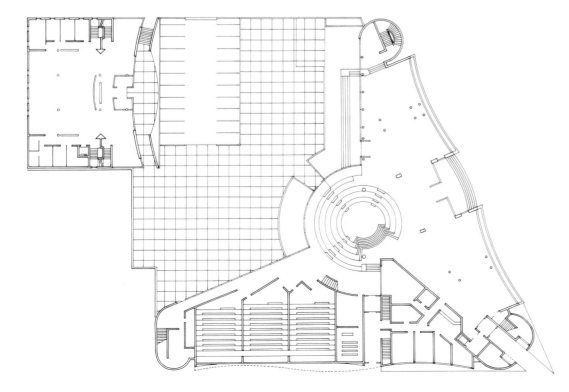

The construction's main
facade has an
undulating design
facing the road,
featuring two
tympanums, one made
of stone to represent
Cartesian rigour,
the other of glass to
symbolise the mystery
of faith.

The building interiors give a sense of the kind of co-operation, communication and knowledge that brings people together.

Control of natural-artificial light allows the interior spaces to be opened up to the world.

Institute of Science and Technology

La Roche-sur-Yon, France

Back in the XIXth century, an old hospital (alongside a prison that is still there today) used to stand on the site where this new building is situated along the city's ring road. The main feature of this site is that it allows the construction of a rather narrow facade along the road front (about twenty meters long), which acts as a pedestrian entrance and, at the same time, allows vehicles to go in and out of the building.

The building brief also specified the construction of a Technical College and Business School on the same site, as well as a separate multi-purpose room for putting on entertainment or organising meetings for the local community. These three functions flow together in a large lobby providing access to all three.

A preliminary analysis of these design constraints, which the architectural design was to be geared around, persuaded Denis Laming to create a distinctly long, cone-shaped piece of architecture, whose overhang onto the boulevard seems to project out protectively towards students and visitors.

It was most important not to create any visual impact on a facility like the prison, which, by its very nature, is designed to be isolated. This meant that the various building functions had to be arranged in a rather unusual way. In any case, the cantilever roof and serigraphed glass combine to create a sort of thin screen that blocks out the prison but lets in light and opens up alternative views.

The building has a slim, practical design that successfully expresses the kind of studies it will have to host. All the pathways feature the kind of efficiency and practicalness that the architecture embodies in its rigorously inviting structures.

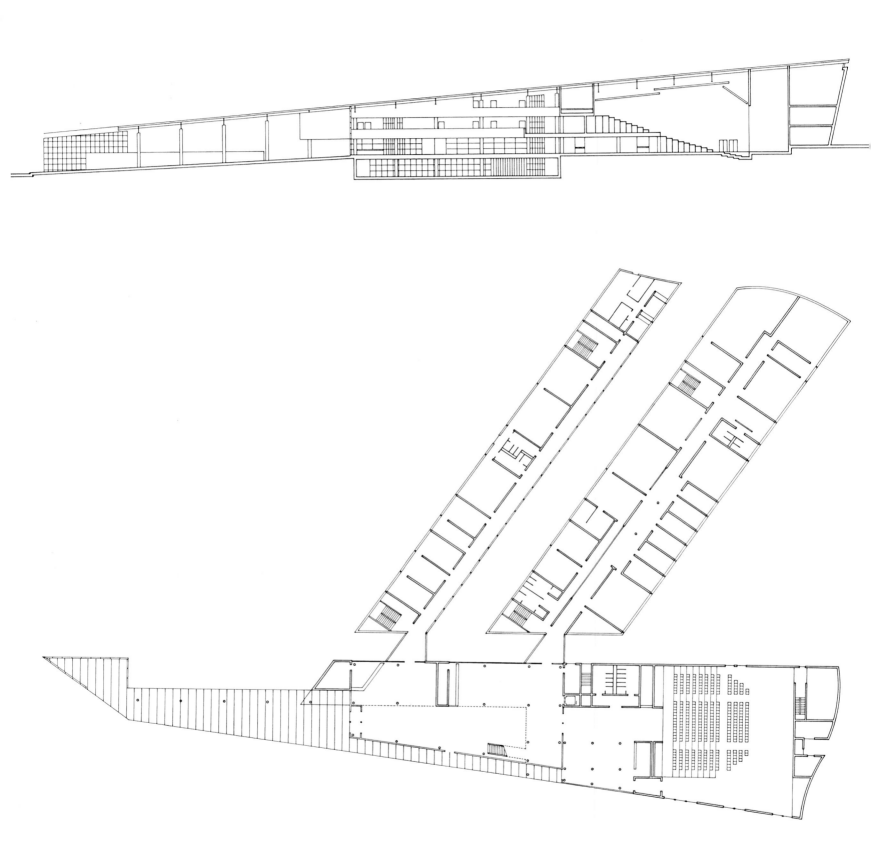

Two views of the building interiors, showing details of the structures.

The teaching spaces are geared to maximum efficiency and practicality to allow the studies to be carried out.

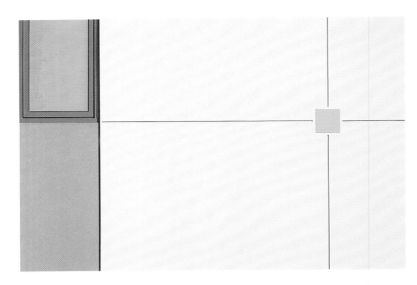

Scienceland

Shanghai, China

Invited to take part in a competition to design a science museum for Shanghai, Denis Laming created an architectural form which is more the physical embodiment of a concept than an ordinary structure.

He basically began with an idea of space whose innovation and creativity evoke a feeling of universal nature and life, arranged in a carefully gauged layout of functions such as intelligence, the future, and infancy. This succession of concepts has been stylistically rendered in a series of architectural levels which rise up and stretch out to form the main architectural structure.

The new Museum slots neatly into the Pudong district's town-planning scheme. It follows the lie of the land and oblique flow of the canal, whose bank has actually been further embellished in landscaping terms. Its structures subtly interact dialectically with those of the Government Building.

The overall architectural image of the new facility is geared to the basic planning scheme designed for Futuroscope Park in Poitiers. In actual fact, they really only share the same functional premises, bearing in mind that both complexes are designed with scientific progress and the future in mind. Apart from this evident analogy, the "Scienceland" Museum in Shanghai is designed along quite different lines to Futuroscope. Here the idea of scientific progress and the quality of life it entails are embodied in a distinctly contained, interiorised and implicit work of architecture. Far from instantly catching the eye, its plastic forms slowly emerge on the horizon like a natural efflorescence. Laming tells us that "it is a sort of logo or sloping cosmic semi-plane", mirroring the mysterious structures of the cosmos. Its architectural compactness entrenches it in the ground, from which it rises up obliquely through a kind of subterranean life force, almost reminiscent of the way thought is projected into the depths of the universe. The microcosm mirrors the macrocosm and is mirrored in it, as a wise old Oriental proverb tells us. A work of conceptual architecture, Denis Laming's Scienceland points towards the latest frontier of a new form of architecture in which science plays a guiding rather than conquering role.

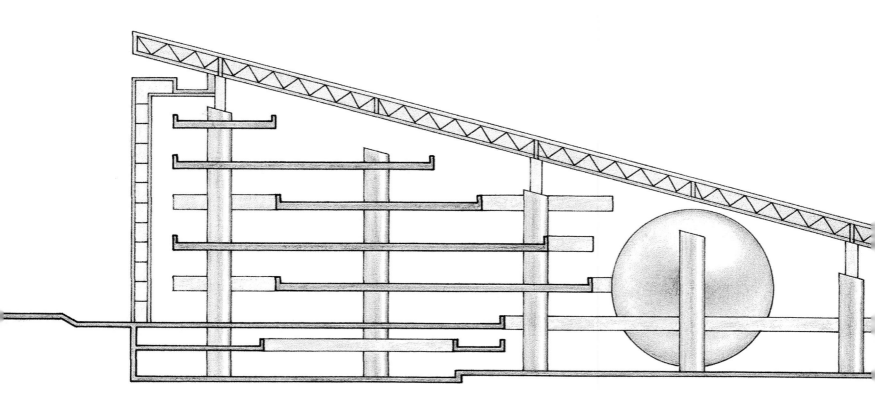

Once again in this
project, basic geometric
figures knit into a clever
architectural design
supported by a high-
tech structure to create
an image forcefully
expressing the idea of
science projected into
the future.

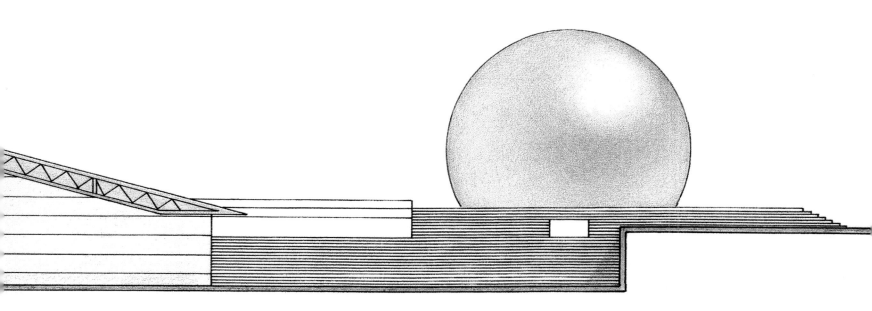

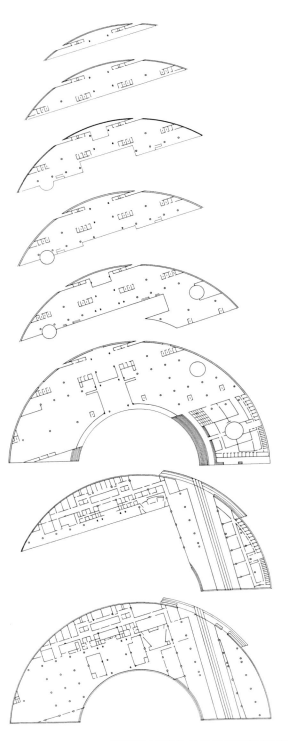

The building's site plan embodies the dynamic force of a scientific approach increasingly based on vision and visual communication.

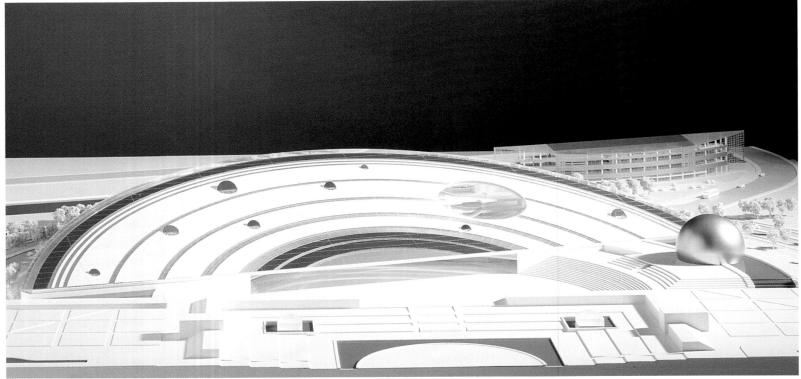

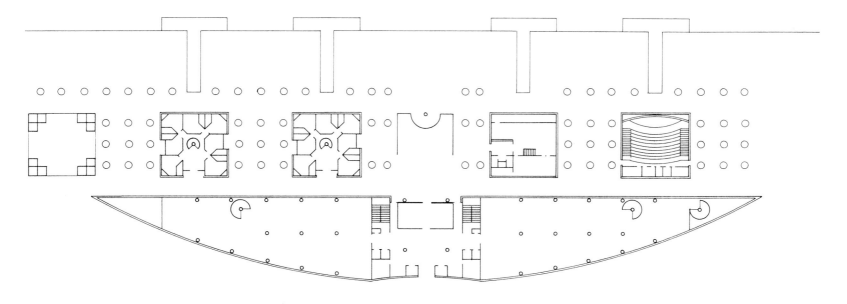

The facade's
clear-cut image
is matched by
the horizontal layout
of spaces, again
geared to maximum
functionality.

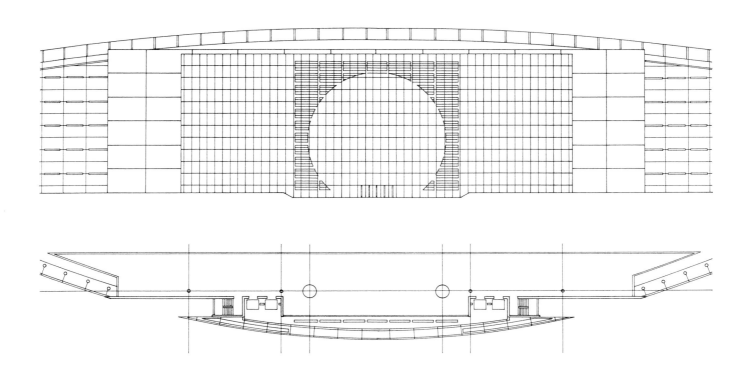

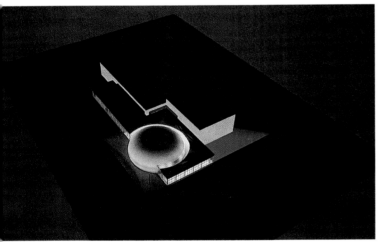

Pacific Science Center and Boeing Imax®

Seattle, USA

The project to extend the Pacific Science Center in Seattle is another "representation" or, if you like, "staging" of science and nature. Denis Laming has used architecture to symbolise knowledge and the kind of mastery of design that shapes the forms - images - of modern-day culture and that of the near future.

Science is represented by a quadrangular geometric form and nature by the egg-shape it spawns - a clear allusion to life as it grows and evolves from inert material. This "emerging entity" turns into an architectural design embodying both the building's overall meaning and its function as both a place of learning and enjoyment. It is really a theater as we can see from its internal auditorium.

The staging process actually begins with the outside architecture, which, as in all of Laming's work, is not just a transient set design, but actually physically embodies its inside contents. The glass ring surrounding and supporting the "egg" creates a sort of "aura" both during the day and at night, multiplying the building's meanings as the idea of emergence, growth and blossoming is emphasised by its structure which appears to flutter freely in the air. The circular ramps winding beneath the ring accentuate this sense of levitation: they lead visitors down into the main hall, drawing them away from the upward thrust of the outside into a more subterranean, chthonic environment, its exact opposite.

Originally designed by Minoru Yamasaki as a cloister, the new design fits in neatly with the existing architecture, extending its force field and opening it up towards the city.

The project focuses on
tightly-knit architectural
symbolism, in which the
forms weave together
into an image charged
with semantic energy.

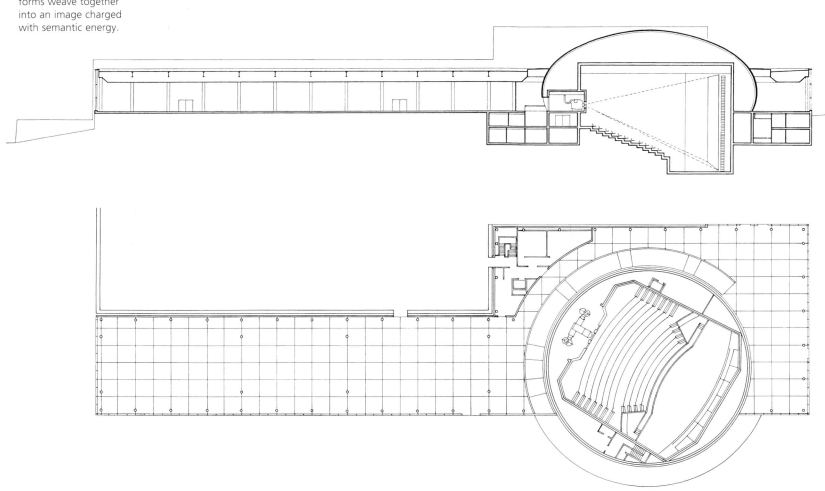

A series of views of the model underlining the structural layout and interaction between interior and exterior.

An outside image
clearly showing the
stylistic force of the
architecture.

Omnivest Business Park

Denver, USA

Denis Laming has combined maximum functionality with the typical stylistic qualities of his architecture in this large complex designed for the purposes of communication, interaction, and exchange.

The complex's circular site plan nicely embodies the way ideas and projects circulate; on a vertical level, the sheer intricacy of the architectural features evokes the waste, differences, and oscillations characterising the world in which we now live.

Omnipark is devised to be a sort of business campus globally integrating trade, technology, education, and progress in life. Against the magnificent backdrop of the Rocky Mountains, it slots into the Denver landscape like a sort of cornerstone of the city's Southeast Business Corridor.

The architecture's structures and construction techniques reinforce the sophisticated technology used for the activities taking place inside the Business Park: the infrastructural systems include high-tech energy generation appliances for data transmission and communication purposes, drawing on teleports, optic fibres, and satellite facilities.

The campus is designed to host two million square feet of office space, multimedia productions, teleconference facilities, and staff training services. This, of course, includes hotels, restaurants, refreshment and entertainment facilities, shops, a child care service, and other facilities.

The Omnivest Business Park in Denver has been described as a "glass icon" and "futuristic" design. The allusion to the iconic force of Futurist-type architectural features is nothing new in Denis Laming's work. But this needs to be explained more clearly. Emphasising the scenographic side of his works is bound to give only a "superficial" idea of the architecture. But if this is intended to bring out its representative qualities, encompassing not just the structures' most immediate contents but also their cultural connotations, general groundings and projections into the future, this injects these works of architecture with stylistic features, concrete contents, and cultural implications.

This also applies to Laming's latest projects as they strive to meet the functional demands of buildings without abandoning a stylistically eloquent architectural idiom. This is the field on which architecture's fate will be battled out, as can clearly be seen from the Denver Omnipark.

This page and opposite page, a sequence of views of the model illustrating its site plan.

This page and opposite page, other views of the complex, clearly showing the dynamic layout of structures and spaces.

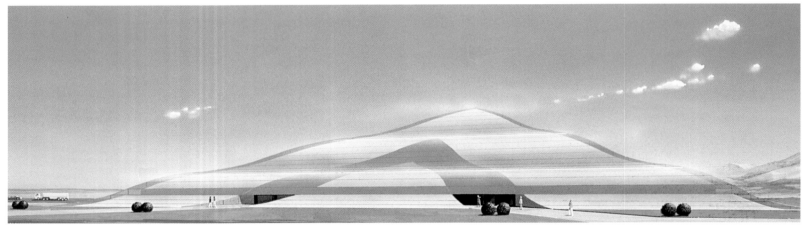

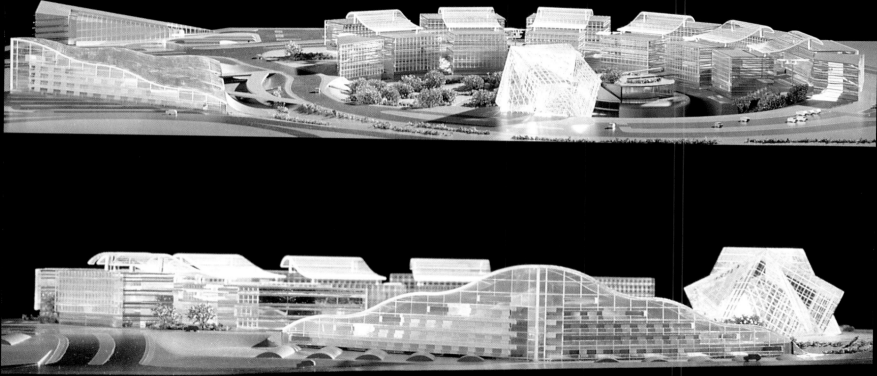

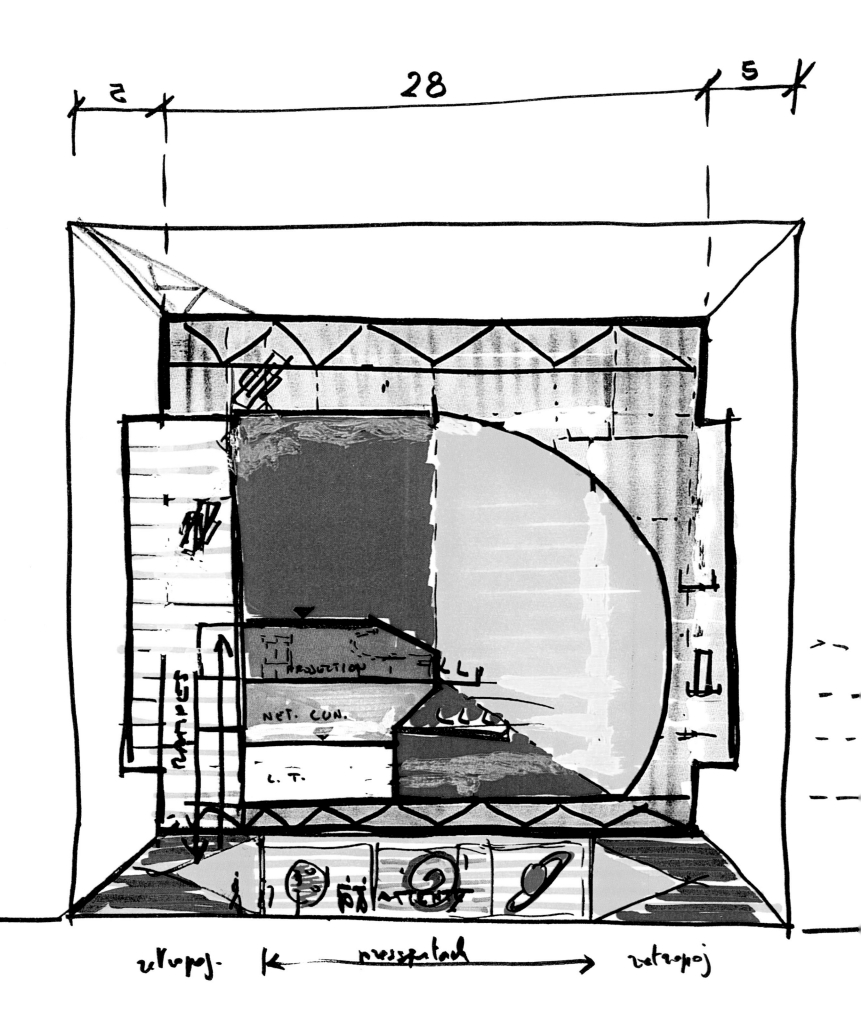

Atlantis

Poitiers, France

The Atlantis building to the north-east of Futuroscope Park is designed to hold an Imax® 3D Dynamique film theater with a spherical screen. The building is constructed out of two volumes: a hypercube and a cylinder combined together in a system of invisible tensile forces.

The hypercube is a geometric representation of the fourth dimension. As opposed to a three-dimensional cube which is an orthogonal projection of a square, a hypercube results from the projection of a three-dimensional cube in the direction of all its sides along a fourth dimension. In actual fact, as Denis Laming points out, "the hypercube evokes the way a number of interlocking universes are combined together, an endless hierarchy of universes, an infinite number of civilisations. It evokes the uncreated world, time without either a beginning or end, cubic crystal spectography, a crystal structure."

The second cylindrical volume is supposed to be an icon to the world of entertainment, the circus, and film industry. It is a sort of staging of the imaginary, whose centre is occupied by the Imax® 3D "Race to Atlantis" film with motion simulators like a levitating drum inside the hypercube. It calls to mind luminous magnetic fields, from which it seems to be suspended.

This description is reminiscent of the kind of science fiction which is closely based on scientific facts, which it is ready to project into an interior world, where enthusiasm and fear combine to form stylistically elaborate compositions. It is actually in cartoon strips more than books or films that we find the seeds of the boldest architectural designs; and Laming's architectural idiom seems to provide a foretaste of a future that it actually creates rather than scrutinises, bringing about a sort of metamorphosis.

This is a spectacle within a spectacle. At night the cylinder's luminous dynamism creates a sense of continual rotation, like gravitation waves, bands, and spectral codes. The structural-iconic tension remains invisible, but it can actually be perceived in the spatial relations, optical illusions, and shifting images.

The architecture mirrors, relates, and represents through its own narrative structures and codes. But it is also penetrated, controlled, and experienced according to the canons of entertainment that both amuses us and makes us think. The building's very name is mythically allusive: it harks back to the fate of a civilisation shrouded in mystery, lost for ever just as it was about to touch a future which we actually now inhabit.

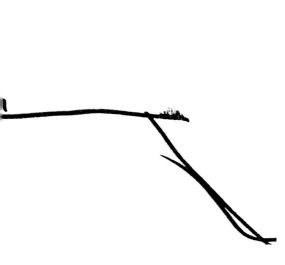

Atlantis will house an Imax® 3D Dynamic film theater with a spherical screen measuring 25 m in diameter.

The building will rise up 30 m above ground level and is constructed out of a hypercube and cylinder fused into a network of invisible tensions.

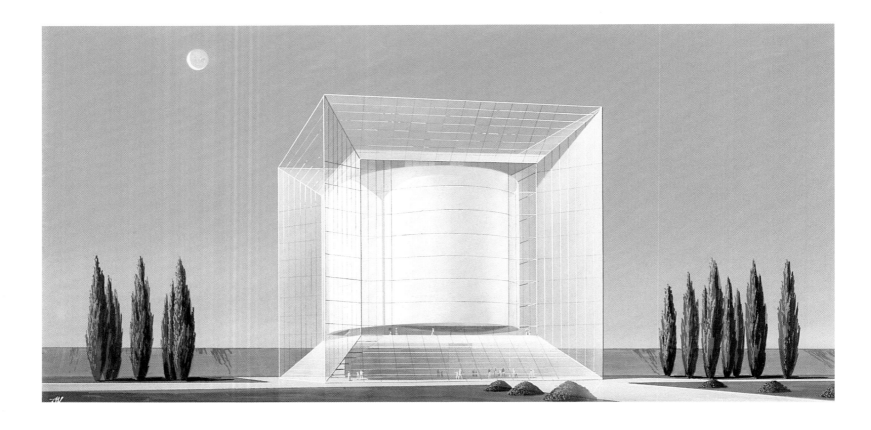

Night-time view of
hypercube and cylinder.

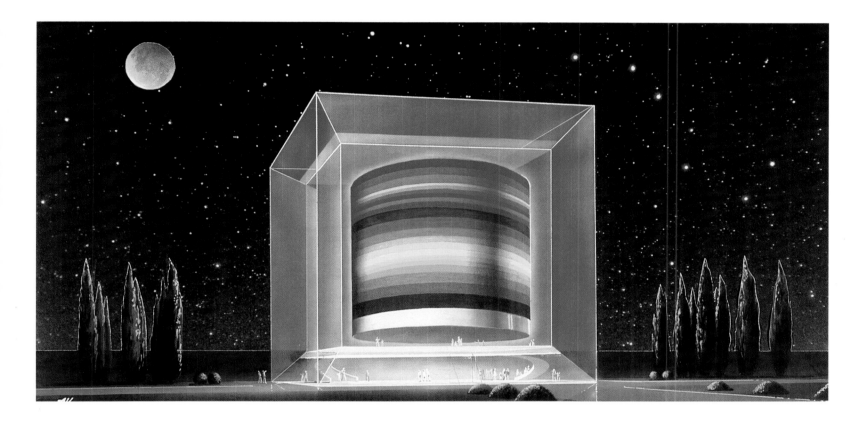

Ecumenical Center
for the Study of Religious Images

Poitiers, France

The building is designed to host an exhibition center for the study of religious images, a chaplaincy and place of worship. It is actually a multi-purpose space that can be adapted by adjusting the position of its mobile walls.

"If God is invisible", Denis Laming points out, "He can only be represented through the figure of Christ". This explains why the building has a cross-shaped plan, a figure that reoccurs in several other architectural features.

In any case, the architecture forms a kinetic sequence. Viewed from afar, the wide glass partition is a "meaningful" landmark. Entering the heart of the building, its architectural image - structures, stairs, chiaroscuro effects, opacity, and transparency - grows gradually more intense. The alternating combination of light and shadow creates a sense of permanent transition between the visible and invisible, as if the light of revelation had suddenly struck after a period of groping around in the dark.

Vertically mounted mobile partitions close off the space as required, like pavilions on which the large veil concealing the holy area hangs.

The roof represents the magical Garden of Eden, whose carefully arranged, painted vegetation converges towards the Tree of Life, standing forever out of reach, represented by a cedar tree (the tree that never loses its leaves). The roof is lit up at all times. The square plan, which is actually a horizontal projection of the glass partition, the hanging garden, and the glass partition itself, symbolise the earth, man, and human spirit.

This is a XXIst-century church built in the absence of substance through its extremely simple site plan (free from fancy forms) and a design playing entirely on space and transparency. Glass cladding beneath the fountain lets in light to mark the Holy Spirit's descent from the heavens, bathing Christ's head. On the inside, the light is opalescent except near the cross, diffusing semi-darkness into the basement of the main hall and turning it into a sort of crypt shrouded in mystery.

Denis Laming has obviously put a lot of work into this construction. The project for a building with revelationary religious connotations is the hardest challenge architecture can face, as Laming well knows. He is also well aware of the effort a challenge like this requires at a time of great technological revolution and ideological crisis, forcing architecture to come to terms with history, calling for a carefully balanced analysis of the past and visionary approach to a future gasping to be filled with meaning. Patiently working with these conflicting forces has resulted in the emergence of a contemporary architectural design based more on strength of will than on firm analytical foundations.

Laming's architecture moves with sure-footed confidence across this terrain, to the point of being a beacon lighting up the way to the changes that lie ahead.

These pages site plan, plan and section of the building, showing the symbolic contents of this architecture which, here more than ever, takes on meanings that contain it and, at the same time, move beyond it.

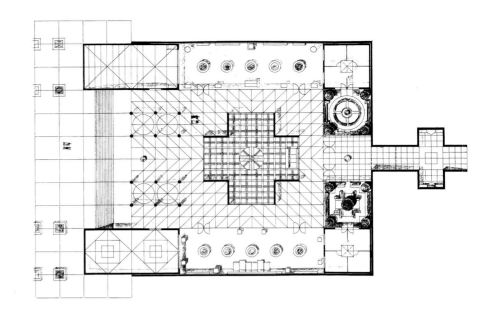

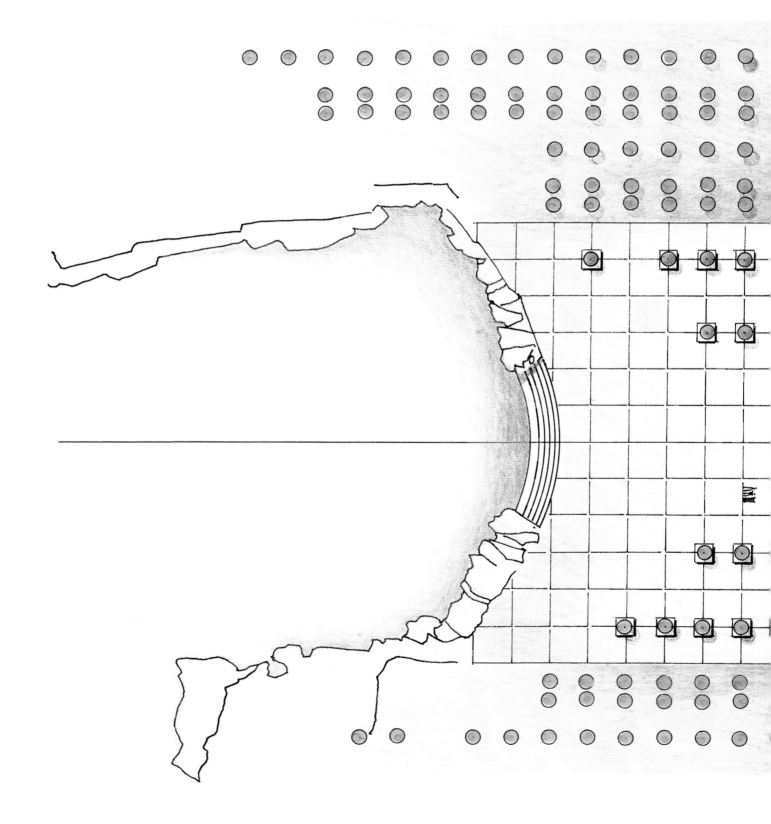

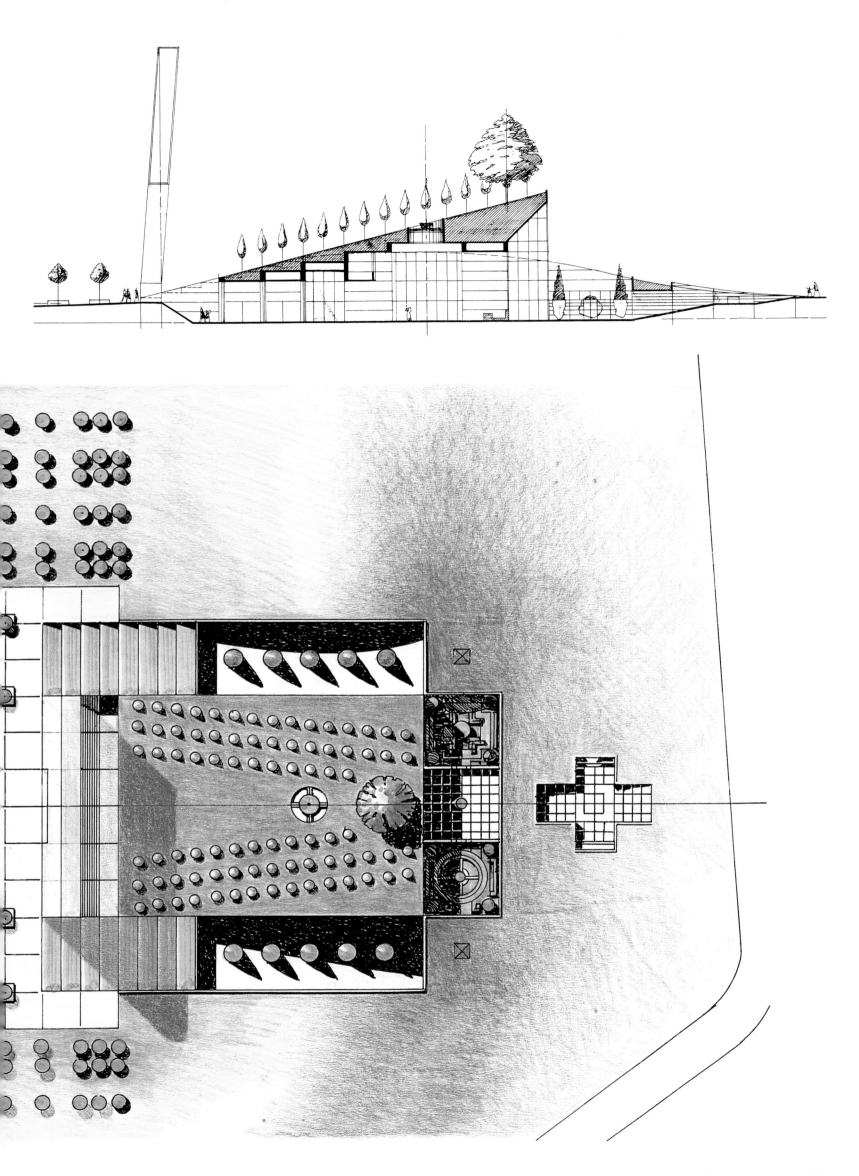

List of Works

1978

TOWN HOUSE
Residence
Saint Cloud, Paris

HUNTING RETREAT
Residence
Sologne, Loiret

CREDIT MUTUEL
Bank Interior
Loudun, Vienne

EQUESTRIAN CENTRE
Rehabilitation of Sports
Facilities
Moncontour, Vienne

STUCKI HOUSE
Residence
Etang la Ville, Paris

GYMNASIUM
Sports Facility
Les Trois Moutiers, Vienne

CULTURAL CENTER
Theater
Poitiers, Vienne

FERME GERMAIN
Residence
Menestreau en Villette, Loiret

PROTECTED
ENVIRONMENTAL ZONE
Urban Development
Vienne

1979

ARJOMARI
Office and Multimedia Center
Paris (interior)

HOSPITAL
Restaurant
Loudun, Vienne

LOUDUN 2000
Shopping Center
Loudun, Vienne

CENTRE LECLERC
Shopping Center
Poitiers, Vienne

ROMAN CHURCHES
Restoration
Vienne

C.E.S. 240
Primary School
Saint Jean de Sauves, Vienne

CENTRE LECLERC
Shopping Center
Fontenay le Comte, Vienne

CULTURAL CENTER
Community Hall
Saint Jean de Sauves, Vienne

1980

CENTRE JACQUES BREL
Community Hall
Mantes la Ville, Vienne

MUSEE ACADIEN
Museum Restoration
La Chaussée, Vienne

VILLAGE DE VACANCES
Residence
Moncoutour, Vienne

1981

CENTRE CULTUREL
Community Hall
Lusignan, Vienne

1982

C.E.S. 300
Primary School
Saint Sever, Calvados

C.E.S. 900
Extension to College
Loudun, Vienne

CENTRE LECLERC
Extension to Shopping Center
Poitiers, Vienne

ROIFFE GOLF COURSE
Rehabilitation of Club House
Roiffé, Vienne

1983

CENTRE LECLERC
Shopping Center
Loudun, Vienne

TOWN CENTER
Pedestrian Streets
Loudun, Vienne

1984

FUTUROSCOPE PARK
Urban Planning and General
Conception
Futuroscope, Poitiers

1986

FUTUROSCOPE PAVILION
Exposition Hall
Futuroscope, Poitiers

CHILDREN'S WORLD
Attractions
Futuroscope, Poitiers

1987

THEATRE ALFA –
NUMERIQUE
Amphitheater and Aquatic
Stage
Futuroscope, Poitiers

KINEMAX
Imax® Theater
Futuroscope, Poitiers

L'EUROPE
Restaurant
Futuroscope, Poitiers

CRISTAL
Restaurant
Futuroscope, Poitiers

TETRAPAK
Attractions
Futuroscope, Poitiers

LAC 1
Aquatic Stage
Futuroscope, Poitiers

OFFICES AND
MAINTENANCE
BUILDINGS
Futuroscope, Poitiers

SHOPPING ARCADES
Futuroscope, Poitiers

1989

DURAS CASTLE
Interior Rehabilitation
Duras, Lot et Garonne

PUY DU FOU
Open-air Amphitheater
Vendée

INTERNATIONAL
PROSPECTIVE INSTITUTE
Technology Center
Futuroscope, Poitiers

C.N.E.D. MULTIMEDIA
CENTER HEADQUATERS
Studio for Audiovisual
Productions for Tele-learning
Futuroscope, Poitiers

COMMUNICATION
PAVILION
Auditorium and Projection
Theater
Futuroscope, Poitiers

RESTAURANT
Futuroscope, Poitiers

DYNAMIC SHOWSCAN
Simulator
Futuroscope, Poitiers

PALAIS DES CONGRES 1
Conference Center
Futuroscope, Poitiers

C.G.I.
Office Buildings
Futuroscope, Francee

HOTEL D'ANGLETERRE
2 Star + Hotel
Futuroscope, Poitiers

1990

BUREAUX RELAIS
Office Buildings
Loudun, Vienne

TELEPORT
Telecommunication Center
Futuroscope, Poitiers

GEMINI
Student Housing
Futuroscope, Poitiers

HOPITAL RENAUDOT
Extension and Restructuring
Loudun, Vienne

360° CINEMA
Projection Hall
Futuroscope, Poitiers

GYMNASIUM 1 AND 2
Sports Facilities
Futuroscope, Poitiers

HOTEL FUTUROSCOPE
Residence and Restaurant
Futuroscope, Poitiers

IBIS
2 Star Hotel
Futuroscope, Poitiers

1991

OMNIMAX
Hemispherical Projection Hall
Futuroscope, Poitiers

ASTERAMA
Office Building
Futuroscope, Poitiers

H.L.M. 2
Student Housing
Futuroscope, Poitiers

1992

MAGIC CARPET
Imax® Theater
Futuroscope, France

AQUASCOPE
Interactive Theater
Futuroscope, Poitiers

PANASONIC
Theater
Futuroscope, Poitiers

1994

WATER TOWER
Loudun, Vienne

I.C.E.S.
Catholic University
La Roche-sur-Yon, Vendée

SOLIDO
3D Theater
Futuroscope, Poitiers

VIENNE PAVILION
THEATER
Media Wall and Simulator
Futuroscope, Poitiers

FRANTOUR – AQUATIS
3 Star Hotel
Futuroscope, Poitiers

MORPHEE
Student Housing
Futuroscope, Poitiers

1995

IMAGE STUDIO
Attraction Pavilion
Futuroscope, Poitiers

1996

JURISCOPE – JURIPOLE
International Juridical
Information Center
Futuroscope, Poitiers

CAMPANILE
Hotel et Restaurant
Futuroscope, Poitiers

ALTAIR
Student Housing
Futuroscope, Poitiers

IMAX® 3D
Imax® Theater
Futuroscope, Poitiers

SP2MI
C.N.R.S. Research Center
and University
Futuroscope, Poitiers

PALAIS DES CONGRES 2
Conference Center
Futuroscope, Poitiers

1997

METEOR
3 Star Hotel
Futuroscope, Poitiers

I.S.T.V.-E.G.C.
Institute of Science
and Technology
La Roche-sur-Yon, vendee

I.C.E.S. UNIVERSITY
LIBRARY
La Roche sur Yon, Vendée

CYBER AVENUE
Amusement Arcade
Futuroscope, Poitiers

1998

A.F.P.A.
Life Long Learning Center
Futuroscope, Poitiers

IMAGIQUE
Theater and Restaurant
Futuroscope, Poitiers

PACIFIC SCIENCE
CENTER
Boeing Imax Theater
Seattle, Washington State, U.S.A.

OMNIVEST
Business Center
Denver, Colorado State, U.S.A.

T.G.V. STATION
Futuroscope, Poitiers
(under construction)

PARK PLAZZA
4 Star Hotel
Futuroscope, Poitiers

IMAX ATLANTIS
3D Dynamic Theater
Futuroscope, Poitiers
(under construction)

SURAVENIR ASSURANCES
Headquarters
Nantes, Loire Atlantique
(under construction)

MATHEMATICS
LABORATORIES
Research University
Futuroscope, Poitiers

L.E.A.
Aerodynamic Studies Laboratory
and Research Center
Futuroscope, Poitiers

ACKERLEY EXHIBIT
GALLERY
Pacific Science Center,
Museum Extension
Seattle, Washington State,
U.S.A.

C.N.E.D. HEADQUARTERS
National Tele-learning Center
Futuroscope, Poitiers

CEGETEL
Company Headquarters
Futuroscope, Poitiers

T.D.R.
Office Building
Futuroscope, Poitiers

DELTA
Office Building
Futuroscope, Poitiers

PARK PLAZA
Office Building
Futuroscope, Poitiers

FUTURISTIC OCEAN LINER
France
(conception)

1999

THESSALONIKI
TECHNOLOGY MUSEUM
Science Museum
and Planetarium
Thessaloniki Island, Greece
(conceptual phase)

COMPETITION
FOR BRITAIR
Headquarters
Morlaix, Finistère

COMPETITION FOR
THEATER MULTIPLEX
AND SIMULATOR
Amnéville, Moselle

URBAN DEVELOPMENT
DESIGN COMPETITION
Oberhausen, Germany

HIGT-TECH OFFICE
BUILDING
Futuroscope, Poitiers

CENTER FOR RELIGIOUS
IMAGES
Futuroscope, Poitiers

RETREAT HOUSE
La Roche-sur-Yon, France

Biography

Denis Laming founded his firm in Paris as a very young architect in 1978 and quickly established himself as a talented architect creating expressive public architecture for cultural and educational institutions. He is acclaimed for his work as chief architect and urban planner of Futuroscope in France featuring 18 state-of-the-art theaters, a university, research laboratories, and conference facility. Futuroscope received 3 million visitors this year and Laming is currently building there a facility to house the latest 3D image technology with motion simulators as well as a futuristic train station to cater for the fastest train on earth due to open in 1999.

Other projects he is currently working on include The Valley Forge Museum of the American Revolution, The Technology Museum, Thessaloniki Greece, and an Aquascenie for the city of Paris.

Laming is recognized internationally as a specialist in anticipating future needs of urban environments and is known for bringing a fresh perspective to challenging projects by designing unique, communicative, interactive architecture. Laming is also credited by European architecture critics for initiating futurism within the Post-Modern movement. He describes his work as follows: "From the cut-glass of the Kinemax at Futuroscope to the injecting of fresh life into old monuments, I have tried to take the architect as we usually see him and transform him into a sort of alchemist capable of blending together technology and the arts in a subtle interplay of dreaming and imagination. Only the latter won't betray us, as Ionesco once wrote. Luck, hard work, and the support of all those who have shown faith in me from the very beginning, have allowed me to develop these ideas and create architecture combining the symbolic and concrete, the strength of matter and the power of myth. Architecture anchored to reality but designed in the stars."

Collaborators
1978-1999

Architect Team
Marc Faure, Project Architect
José-Luis Crespo, Project Architect
Cecilia Schubert, Project Architect

Valérie Caron
Christophe Chauvin
Josselin Fleury
Denis Muet
Isabelle Ossent
Anne Peyroux
Etienne Raczynski
Christine Simonin
Eric Vovos

Administrative Team
Thais Trobaugh
May Moreau
Thérèse Cau
Sophie Cuau
Frédérique Joly
Florence Fontani

Collaborators
Claude Alain
Jean Louis Courtois
Alain Cuvelier
Christian Douchet (Abex)
Christian Guillebault (Soneco)
François Heydacker (Outside)
Igor Hilbert (Betecs)
Jacques Hourcade
Bernard Jaunay
Jacques Labyt
Philippe Libre
André Pizon
Pierre Sallaberry (Soneco)
François Scolaro (TBS)
Dan Tatusesco
Jean Louis Vacher (Outside)
Adrian Visan

Collaborating Architectural Firms
Pierre Tuloup Architects
Callison Architecture
The Crosby Group Architecture